Backpacking
With Your Dog

Richard Lerner, DVM

Illustrations by Leigh Ellis

Menasha Ridge Press
Birmingham, Alabama

In Memory of Maggie,
    the best trail companion a man could have hoped for

Acknowlededements

I'd like to thank Mike Jones of Menasha Ridge Press for asking me to write this book, and Dr. Sandra Sawchuk, not only an excellent veterinarian but an excellent teacher, for her help on the manuscript. Thanks also to Beverly Lerner for her expertise in syntax and grammar. As always, C. E. Black has been an invaluable source of support and wisdom, not to mention the photographer for these drawings.

Printed in the United States of America
Published by Menasha Ridge Press
First edition, first printing

Illustrations by Leigh Ellis
Text design by Carolina Graphics Group

Menasha Ridge Press
3169 Cahaba Heights Road
Birmingham, Alabama 35243

Contents

Before You Leave Home

It's spring. The trees are beginning to bud, the temperatures are in the high seventies, and it's time to go camping. Take the dogs—it is a chance to go on vacation without suffering those pangs of guilt you normally experience when you put your loyal pal in a boarding kennel or leave her with the dog-sitter. No more sad eyes staring, imploring, "Please, pleeeez, take me with you." Instead, you get the bounding steps, the wagging tail, and that expression dog owners recognize as a smile (though our more skeptical friends tell us we are only anthropomorphizing).

I have two dogs I take hiking with me. I consider them ideal outdoor dogs, though they are both different. Maggie is an Australian Cattle Dog, a highly intelligent animal capable of performing complex herding tasks. She is very much in tune with what I expect of her, which makes her an excellent trail dog. And while Emma, a hound cross obtained at the humane society, is not as "intelligent" as Maggie, she makes up for it in athletic ability. She loves to hike and swim, and seems nearly indefatigable. What's more, my dogs are good company.

It's fun to bring a dog on a camping trip, especially when you are traveling alone.

It's fun to bring the dog on a camping trip, especially when you're travelling alone. You feel safer. You can play Frisbee. You can read to your dog. I recommend *The Literary Dog*, Jeanne Schinto, editor. It has good contemporary dog stories. (Be selective in what you read to your dog—some of these stories can be depressing.) Jack London tales are always canine favorites, as are James Herriot's dog stories. And when you're bored, putting a

dollop of peanut butter on your dog's upper lip is good for five minutes of entertainment.

Love for the outdoors and love for animals are linked. There is no better way to experience this connection than by taking a trip with your canine friend. But before you go, it's important to determine whether the trip you're planning is a good idea for both you and your dog.

To Dog It or Not

There are times when it is appropriate to take your dog on a trip, and times when it is best to find a dog-sitter. Though the hikes I've taken with my dogs have been among the most enjoyable experiences of my life, there are places where dogs are a hindrance. Additionally, there are places where an animal's well-being is endangered.

There are places where an animal's well-being is endangered.

Are you going to a National Park? Unless you're planning to stay in the campgrounds parked in the Airstream while Country and Western music wafts in from the other RV's and caravans, you may as well leave your dog at home. It's not within the scope of this guide to examine why people vacation this way, but should you find yourself within the confines of a National Park, your dog will spend his vacation restricted to one of these glorified parking lots. Dogs are not allowed on trails in National Parks. If you are thinking of circumventing this rule, you will get in a heap of trouble, with nothing but an "I-told-you-so" from me. Many National Parks have kennels nearby. If you choose this option, keep in mind that your dog will be in contact with dogs from all over the nation. Do you know the standards to which these kennels are kept?

And forget fishing. Dogs and hooks have an amazing affinity, and the animals usually run in the water and scare all the fish away. I never catch fish when my dogs are along.

Is she conditioned for the trek that you've planned?

There are additional considerations when deciding whether to take your dog. Is she conditioned for the trek that you've planned? Has she been acclimated to carrying her pack? If you exercise with your dog, chances are that it will be easier on the dog than on you, given the average dog's superior athleticism. On the other hand, if your dog sits on the sofa while you run forty miles a week, you will probably be disappointed in her performance, as she lags behind, plodding her way towards exhaustion and heat stroke. Just as you shouldn't plan on hiking a long-distance trail without getting in shape, you shouldn't expect any different from your dog. It's as satisfying to see your dog respond to an athletic challenge as if you had done it yourself.

Things to Consider

Unfriendly People

There are people out there who don't like dogs. These people are generally evil, or at best, highly undesirable elements of society—products of bad breeding. Unfortunately, they look just like you and me. They live for the sake of forming associations with others of their ilk, associations that exist for the sake of complaining about things, like other people's dogs. *Do not argue with these people!* If your dog is bothering them, just apologize and take your critters elsewhere.

As always, prevention is the best cure. Keep your dog on a leash while in populated areas. Do not let him mark his territory on the tires of campers. When in a campground, use the plastic bags you've brought for the purpose of cleaning up after your dog. With the aforementioned evil ones, do not attempt to make light of the situation with such comments as, "I wish I could go in the woods so easily." These people are notoriously humorless, and such attempts are doomed to failure. Suck it up, be polite, and don't let your children mingle with theirs.

Keep your dog on a leash whenever possible.

Before you go hiking, check out whether the area you are exploring is dog-friendly or not, especialy if you plan on staying in a hotel or hostel. Some places forbid dogs from sleeping in their rooms. While this may have been corrected legally in many areas, you may still get a cold reception when you try to keep your dog with you. If you do venture into these areas, just don't plan on bringing him into your room when you stop for a shower.

Legal Considerations

Like all animals, dogs need a health certificate from an accredited veterinarian before crossing state or international lines. Except on airplanes, this rule is rarely enforced (The safety of taking pets on airlines has recently come under scrutiny. Despite the assurances of the carriers, animals are lost, and animals die. My pets travel by car only.) Be aware that an agricultural inspector has the right to see a recent (generally within 10 days) health certificate, the same as if you'd shipped a load of cattle.

Always carry proper documentation of vaccinations.

You should keep your dog current on all vaccinations and always carry proper documentation of vaccinations. Rabies is a growing problem. Different states have different requirements on rabies vaccination schedules, and your dog will pay the price for your noncompliance.

If you own a wolf hybrid (strongly discouraged by the American Veterinary Medical Association), know that many states consider them the same as wolves. If your wolf hybrid bites someone, confinement and observation is not an option; the dog will be "sacrificed," and the head sent to the state laboratory for rabies diagnosis.

All animal bites must be reported to local authorities and to the Department of Health where you live. This is information that could save a life. Human deaths from rabies are extremely rare, and we all have to die, but rabies ain't a nice way to go.

Identification

Make sure your dog has proper identification. Should he get lost, tags on a dog's collar tell where you can be found. Many humane societies offer tags for free or for a nominal charge. These tags ensure that, if your dog is found while you are still away, there will always be somebody there to receive the phone call. I also like the tags for another purpose—should your dog get loose, the sound makes it easier to locate him running through heavy underbrush.

Many humane societies offer tags for free or at a nominal charge.

Increasingly, veterinarians and humane societies are offering implantation of microchips for identification purposes. This is a permanent way of identifying a dog. A small microchip containing an identification code is injected underneath the dog's skin, between the shoulder blades. Implantation hurts no more than a vaccination. The chip, containing a code that is assigned to your dog only, can be read by passing a scanner over the dog. The companies that make the microchips maintain the registry of codes, and the greatest obstacle to universal acceptance of this system is lack of uniformity among the companies. It is hoped that soon the industry will implement a common type of microchip, and that humane societies will be required to have scanners for identifying dogs.

Tattoos are also used for permanent identification of dogs. A dog can wear a tag that indicates that he has a tag or tattoo. A permanently-identified dog is also less likely to be stolen for evil and illicit purposes; i.e. dog fights and laboratory use.

Restraint

In most parks, it is required that dogs be restrained on a leash. While I can't advocate flouting park rules, I realize that some pets will be off leash occasionally. Etiquette demands that dogs be under restraint when there are others around or all the time if they bother the natural plants or animals in any way.

Etiquette demands that dogs be under restraint when there are others around.

A dog on a leash is a safe dog. He will not fall off cliffs or into rapids. But there are places where using

a leash will be difficult—climbing through a rhododendron thicket or scrambling across scree. Act conservatively, and limit your dog's off-leash time to those occasions when it is actually necessary.

Property owners have the right to shoot if the dog is molesting livestock.

Another compelling reason to use a leash is that property owners have the right to shoot a dog on their land if the dog is molesting livestock. As a hunting and herding animal, a dog delights in chasing other animals, often for the sheer fun of it. A dog can inflict serious damage on livestock or cause the animals to hurt themselves when chased.

Also, remember to respect the safety of trail riders. Horses with riders should be given a wide berth. Keeping your dog on a leash and stepping off the trail is for the safety of you and your dog, as well as horse and rider.

When buying a leash, you will want to consider its length. A leash that is too long will end up wrapped around trees, and one that is too short will put your dog underfoot. Retractable leashes are nice for when you need to shorten or lengthen the leash, but I prefer the feel and simplicity of a plain six-foot leather lead.

Naturally, your dog has a collar, a place to attach a leash and the rabies and identification tags. There are several types of collars to choose from. Choke collars have been the mainstay of dog training for years. However, choke collars have been responsible for injuries, both on the trail and at home. These incidents are rare, and many dogs are trained to respond to the tug of a choke collar. If it works for you, and is what you are used to, then stick with it. There are other methods, though.

An alternative to the choke collar is the halter. There are several companies that make these, and they are available at pet supply stores.

It takes much less force to correct a dog by controlling his head than by using exertion on his neck. If you've had trouble training a dog who is unresponsive to the choke collar, try the halter. I have not heard of any halter accidents to date. They cannot cut off breathing the way a choke collar can.

Many dogs who don't mind collars will object to the use of a halter. Most dogs can be made to tolerate it though, at least for part of the day. A halter is not a muzzle; your dog will be able to eat, drink, and bite while wearing it.

If neither of these alternatives is satisfactory, a figure eight harness may be appropriate. Unlike the halter or collar, the figure eight harness can be used

Choke collars have been responsible for injuries, both on the trail and at home.

to lift the dog to safety. However, if your dog carries her own pack, it may interfere with it.

Obedience Training

A trained dog is a happy dog.

Which brings me to another point—a trained dog is a happy dog. A trained dog is less likely to run in front of a car. A trained dog is less likely to cause annoyance to those sub-human clones (see above) that don't like canines. Enroll your dog and yourself in an obedience class. Practice.

Equipment

Your main consideration in outfitting your dog will be the purchase of an appropriate dog pack. There are a variety of packs on the market. On Emma, I use one produced in Golden, Colorado, by Mountainsmith. Maggie uses an old pack made by some now-defunct company. Why these packs?—because they work on my dogs. It's the same with your own backpacks; you may find that a Kelty pack works for you, while a friend swears by Dana.

In addition to the Mountainsmith pack, the most widely available pack is by Eagle Creek, but there are other companies around that make them. I have seen one by a company called Wenaha. Many companies dealing in dogsledding materials also sell dogpacks.

Packs are sold with weight recommendations. My dogs, Maggie and Emma, weigh approximately the same amount, but they differ in height by several inches. If I had chosen their packs based solely on weight, I would have bought the same pack for both dogs. Although Maggie is quite strong, her low height prevents me from putting the same size pack on her that I use on Emma.

Mail-order has taken over the outdoor goods market to a large degree, but I recommend a trip to the store with your dog to try a pack on before purchasing it. This will save you the trouble of having to return a poor-fitting pack.

The pack should have wide, soft straps. One or two straps go under the dog's torso, and one goes around the front of the dog's chest, in front of his legs. Without this front strap, the pack will slide to the rear of the dog; it may slide off. The pack I use on Emma has a Y-strap, which puts only one strap around the dog's underside, yet gives good stabil-

I recommend a trip to the store with your dog to try a pack on before purchasing it.

ity. I carry an extra strap with me. On steep descents I put it from the rear end of the pack around the dogs' haunches or below their tails. This keeps their packs from sliding too far forward.

Emma's pack has lash rings on top. While I wouldn't use these rings to carry anything sharp or heavy, it's not a bad place to attach a windshirt or light raincoat. It will be subjected to the vicissitudes of Emma's behavior, though.

Beast of burden continues to be one of the many roles that dogs play; they are still used to pull and carry. Owners of toy breeds, I trust, will be sufficiently wise not to take their dogs on extended camping trips, unless they plan on carrying them a good part of the way. However, any reasonably athletic dog with normal conformation can be fitted comfortably with a pack.

Any reasonably atheletic dog can be fitted comfortably with a pack.

In general, I would not recommend planning a trip around the idea of using your dog as a pack mule, but rather as a means of pulling his own weight. It is possible to train some dogs, depending on their size and conformation, to be your beasts of burden, although that is not the subject of this book.

A well-conditioned sled dog can carry up to fifty percent of its weight in a pack, but most dogs are neither this strong nor this conditioned. Most dogs, however, should be able to carry a couple of weeks of their own food supply without undue strain.

My dogs carry their own food. Food is easy to pack. It's uniform and low in density, so even if I fill the packs to capacity, they won't be too heavy. This way, I can travel with the satisfaction that my dogs are pulling their own weight. As their burden lightens, I often replace the weight with some of my own gear—dogpacks make great easy access compartments.

Inspect your dog at least twice daily for sores

caused by the pack. Poor fit, uneven balance, or improper strap tension (too tight or too loose) can cause abrasions. If a sore is developing, treat the sore and pad the area underneath the strap with something soft. Old pieces of synthetic fleece, like Synchilla, work well for this. If you let abrasion progress, you could be carrying your dog's pack as well as your own.

Inspect your dog at least twice daily for sores caused by the pack.

Many dogs enjoy lying down in streams or going for a spontaneous swim. Moreover, the low height of a dog puts his pack close to, or in the water when crossing streams. It is best to put items going in the pack inside two heavyweight plastic bags. If your dog likes to roll in vile, foul-smelling dead things, anything in the pack will be subject to this smell. These things usually make well-worn polypropylene smell like a bed of roses. Also, your dog might be sleeping in the tent—be forewarned.

Introducing your Dog to the Pack

Most dogs will not object to a pack any more than a collar. Don't, however, try putting the pack on your dog for the first time when you're at the trailhead beginning a six-day hike. Let her try out the empty pack at home, then on her normal walk, or a short day-hike. If your dog associates her pack with walks, she will doubtless be excited to wear it. But, if she objects violently to the pack, (I've seen dogs chew through the straps), you'll have to go a bit slower.

If your dog associates her pack with walks, she will be excited to wear it.

The pack I use on Emma has to go over the head, but the one I use for Maggie fastens around the chest, making it easier to put on a dog that objects initially to the pack. I'm not against rewarding dogs with treats, and a bit of food that has to be obtained by placing the head through the pack often does wonders. (This also works well for introducing your dog to halters.)

Equipment for the Boat and Car

Some trips call for extensive travel next to whitewater or fast-moving current. Maybe you are taking your dog on a canoe trip. Class II whitewater is all that a dog should be expected to handle, and then only if he is a strong swimmer. In spite of tales of whitewater heroics, dogs do drown. If water is a significant part of your trip, take along a Personal Floatation Device (PFD) for your dog. These are available from whitewater supply companies.

In spite of tales of whitewater heroics, dogs do drown.

And yes, you can get a seat belt harness for your dog. A little while ago, I would have thought that these were ridiculous. But I've seen dogs jump out of moving cars, or get slammed against the windshield in sudden stops.

Other Useful Equipment

Don't forget dishes on your checklist. A Sierra cup (a metal cup with a wire handle) or a similar type vessel should be kept in your easy access area so that you can give your dog frequent drinks of water.

Booties can be a useful thing. These are available from dogsledding sources. If your dog has been properly conditioned, her pads will be tough enough to withstand most insults the ground has too offer, but you might find yourself in terrain where the dog will welcome the extra protection. This is especially true when there is snow and ice on the ground, which can ball up between the pads. A first aid kit, flea spray (when appropriate), and leashes should also be included.

Planning for the Necessities

Water

The first consideration in planning any type of journey is assuring an adequate supply of safe water. Carrying a day's water supply adds eight pounds per person, and I figure on that much as a minimum for a medium-to-large dog that is exerting herself. Dogs actually are much better at maintaining the balance of hydration than humans are. When able, they drink small amounts constantly, not waiting for the next rest stop.

I try to hike near places that have a good, "safe" water source. Some will counter that that there are no such places, but many streams have water quality rated as good-to-excellent. Yes, there is

They drink small amounts constantly, not waiting for the next rest stop.

It's hard to keep a thirsty dog from drinking available water.

Giardia lamblia (an intestinal protozoal parasite) in many of the streams, but it is hard to determine the actual incidence of illness due to *Giardia*. Often an animal will be a carrier with no symptoms. Other times, an animal will be a carrier, but will not shed cysts, the infectious stage, until stressed.

I don't know if humans are more susceptible to *Giardia* than dogs are; as to my knowledge, no controlled studies have been done. Nor has it been determined if infested pets pose a risk to owners. Unbeknownst to many backpackers, the distribution of *Giardia* is actually quite widespread, with a large number of cases coming from urban areas. Besides the general precautions to avoid infestation, I would recommend fastidious hygiene, especially washing the hands with soap before eating. *Giardia* is no fun. I know from whence I speak.

It's hard to keep a thirsty dog from drinking available water. Take this into consideration when you're planning a hike by a stream that is known to be polluted. I avoid taking my dogs near streams that have untreated sewage or chemical pollutants. On the other hand, when hiking by relatively pristine rivers, I let them go into the water at will. It keeps them cool and hydrated.

If you are concerned about the quality of water, you can boil it as you would your own drinking water. The major drawback of this method is cooling time. Chemically treating water is also possible, but dogs may refuse to drink water that tastes too strongly of iodine or chlorine. Water filters of good quality, another option, are relatively inexpensive. Treating water eliminates biological hazards, but the toxic waste dumped in by the paper mill or backyard hazardous waste disposer will remain.

If I know that I won't be passing near water for over ninety minutes, I fill a water bottle for my dogs and allow them to drink at least every hour and a half—more frequently if it's unusually hot or humid. Use your Sierra cup for this purpose.

After establishing that you and your dog won't be dying of thirst, there are other considerations.

Food

Most dogs are fat. Most dog foods are too high in fat and protein, which is turned into fat when it exceeds the dog's daily needs. You can head off into the back country without worrying that your dog's "Hi-Pro Glow" will wear off under the strain of all those extra calories that he is burning off.

Being overweight predisposes your dog to a myriad of problems, including exhaustion, heat stroke, and long-term ill effects on his health. If your dog is conditioned for trekking, he is not overweight. A dog in good flesh has ribs that can easily be felt, barely pressing against his chest, and will have a definite "waist" behind the ribs as you look down on him from above.

If your dog is conditioned for trekking, he is not overweight.

I feed my dogs normally on the days of our average hikes. If we are doing an especially strenuous multi-day trip, I increase their feed by ten percent. Dogs that do strenuous work constantly, such as sled dogs, stock dogs, or dogs that put in lots of regular miles with their owners, will be on a high ration already. For the dog that goes camping a few times a year, a huge increase in calories isn't necessary and can cause an upset stomach.

Storing food can be a problem if your dog eats a lot. Normally, I feed my dogs a reduced-calorie version of a premium dog food. To save space on a long trip, I use the regular version, which has more calories due to a higher concentration of fat. Performance dog foods are even higher in calories, and may be right for your dog. Fat is one of the few things proven to improve the flavor of dog food to dogs.

Dogs have little tolerance for changes in diet.

Dogs, unfortunately, have little tolerance for changes in diet—changes tend to provoke diarrhea. Therefore, several days before a trip, I begin introducing my dogs to the richer food by mixing it with their regular diet, gradually increasing the proportion with each meal. This avoids the diarrhea associated with a sudden diet change. I also take rice when I go camping. I like the carbs, and if the dogs develop diarrhea or upset stomachs from the richer food, a bland diet is best.

Shelter

Figure that he requires the same shelter on the trail that he requires at home.

Meeting your dog's need for shelter is a relatively simple chore; figure that he requires the same shelter on the trail that he requires at home. Dogs need something that can give them respite from the elements. I camp with a tent that has a vestibule and let the dogs sleep in the vestibule. They generally complain, hoping for access to the inner sanc-

tum of the tent. And, if they haven't spent the day slogging through mud, rolling in dead squirrels, or swimming in every hole they could find, I'll let them in.

I would not think of taking my dogs winter camping. They live indoors and have little tolerance for the cold. Arctic breeds, and other dogs that have been habituated to the cold and have adequate means to protect themselves—sleeping in the tent or burrowing in the snow with other dogs—can tolerate winter temperatures for extended periods of time. As my dogs are not used to sleeping at temperatures below 60° F, I take a blanket to keep them warm on cold nights. (A blanket is also comfortable for them to sleep on if the terrain is rough.)

On the Trail

Everything is ready. Your equipment is in order, your dog is in good physical condition, and you're heading off to the most beautiful woods in North America. Before you go, now is a good time to look at some of the things that could go awry. Some things, like fleas and ticks, can cause discomfort; other more serious occurrences may potentially threaten your dog's life.

It doesn't take a Ph.D. in physiology to figure out that hiking in ninety degree weather in ninety percent humidity is not advisable for your heavily-coated Malamute; or that taking a dog through an area laden with rattlesnakes or bears could pose a problem; or that going out in the backwoods during deer hunting season poses something of a risk. But there may be other problems you may not have considered.

Bugs

"Bugs" is inaccurate. The entomologist tells us that the only critters that should be called bugs are the Reduviidae, or "true bugs," like the kissing bug. But you know what I mean. Various six and eight-legged things with mouth parts that, when magnified, look like something from "Aliens." These are the things that make you itch, pass on Lyme disease, and frighten you when they appear suddenly on a piece of your gear. Some individuals avoid the outdoors because of bugs. Having been confined to a tent on their account, I can understand these feelings. But the discomfort caused by insects can be minimized.

Ticks

Of all the bugs that worry the camper, the tick may present the greatest fear. We're not as much worried about the bite as the possibility of infection with a tick-borne disease, especially Rocky Mountain Spotted Fever or Lyme disease. The incidence of ehrlichiosis, another tick-borne disease that can infect both dogs and humans, is also reported to be on the rise.

The existence of Lyme disease in dogs was a source of heated debate for some years, but it has now been shown to infect and cause illness in dogs. If we examine the blood of dogs who live in areas where Lyme disease is prevalent, many of the dogs show evidence of having been exposed to the disease, while very few actually come down with illness.

Lyme disease in dogs is similar to the disease in humans.

Lyme disease in dogs is similar to the disease in humans—fever, malaise, depression, and pain in the joints. Since many dogs have "titers" (antibodies in their blood demonstrating exposure) without having disease, Lyme disease is often diagnosed by, in addition to a positive titer, the above symptoms and response to a certain class of antibiotics. If caught early it can be treated easily with antibiotics. Owners who worry that their dogs are a reservoir for human infection can rest easy—there is no evidence that dogs can transmit Lyme disease to humans.

The deer tick has been recognized as the most important vector of Lyme disease, but all hard ticks of the same genus can carry it. The tick needs to feast on the dog for a period of time before infection occurs, so daily tick checks are effective in preventing disease. You would do well to do the same for yourself.

Daily tick checks are effective in preventing disease.

Veterinary teaching institutions now recommend that dogs who will be exposed to ticks be vaccinated against Lyme disease. This requires a series of two injections. The length of immunity conferred by the vaccine is still uncertain. Fort Dodge, the company manufacturing the vaccine, claims that immunity lasts one year. Given that the tick season is well less than a year in most parts of the world, yearly boosters should be effective after the first series of injections. Those living in warmer climates, however, should stay in touch with their veterinarians as research clarifies these questions.

There is no vaccine for Rocky Mountain Spotted Fever. The signs of the disease are non-specific: listlessness, depression, loss of appetite—the same signs that dogs show for most systemic diseases. They may have diarrhea, vomiting, discharge from the nose and eyes, coughing, and even neurologic signs. Rocky Mountain Spotted Fever can be treated with antibiotics. Because the symptoms of this disease are so general, let your veterinarian know if your dog may have been exposed to ticks.

Controlling a dog's exposure to ticks is the only prevention for Rocky Mountain Spotted Fever. While flea collars receive little respect in the veterinary community, there is a fairly new product, the tick collar, that has been more effective. Its active ingredient is called amitraz.

Mosquitoes

The greatest danger posed by the mosquito is transmission of heartworm disease.

You are familiar with these dreaded beasts. They are how we donate blood to the food chain. To dogs the greatest danger posed by the mosquito is the possible transmission of heartworm disease. The larva of the heartworm are borne by mosquitoes from one dog (or other mammal) to another, where in seven months or so they develop into adults in some of the large vessels of the heart. This leads to heart failure.

Heartworm disease can be treated, but, as the treatment is rather harsh (arsenic-based drugs and possibly heart surgery), prevention is the preferred mode. There is no reason for any dog to get heartworm disease—preventive medicine is extremely safe and 100 percent effective when used properly. It can be given either monthly or daily. Monthly treatment, besides being easier to give, is more forgiving if you are late by a day or so.

You are no doubt familiar with heartworm disease and, if you are taking the time to read this book, you most likely take your dog in for yearly visits to the veterinarian. Dogs should be tested each year prior to recommencing the preventative medicine. While this is less of an issue with those using the Heartgard monthly pill (ivermectin), it is a necessity for those using the daily pill, or the Interceptor monthly pill, as those medicines can precipitate a dangerous reaction. It's good to have a yearly check in any case, in order to nip an infestation in the bud, in case you have been lax in giving the preventative.

Fleas

What nasty, vile, little beasties! If you've ever had a flea bite, you know they make mosquito bites seem pleasant by comparison. If your dog is allergic to the saliva, fleas can make the poor animal crazy as he scratches himself bald, tears his flesh, and rolls around in pure misery.

If you want to control fleas, you not only need to control them on the dog, but also in the environment. You can't do this on a camping trip, but you can do it at home by treating your house and yard, as well as your dog.

The problem with many dogs is that they are allergic to flea saliva. This causes the intense itching associated with the bite. Flea Allergy Dermatitis is a complicated problem and requires more care than an occasional spraying. Dogs can scratch themselves raw, lose most of their hair, and set themselves up for more skin problems. Don't say, "It's just fleas." These dogs need prompt veterinary attention.

Many dogs are allergic to flea saliva.

There are many flea control products on the market. Fleas are big money makers in the veterinary profession. Ultrasonic collars, vitamin B, and even conventional flea collars are useless in preventing fleas, despite the claims made by manufacturers. So is feeding your dog garlic. Many veterinarians sell flea collars only because the demand for them is so heavy. Nearly every company that makes veterinary products or pharmaceuticals also has a product that they claim to be the latest, be-all and end-all in flea control.

There are different methods for attempting to control fleas. Flea and tick sprays will lessen your dog's parasite load. Sprays made from pyrethrins, a derivative of the chrysanthemum plant, are the least toxic of the sprays that do any good. These sprays can be applied as often as every day.

Flea and tick sprays will lessen your dogs parasite load.

The most economical approach is to buy fly repellent sprays used for horses. These should have either pyrethrins or permethrin, a synthetic pyrethrin, as their active ingredient. Along with killing fleas and ticks, these agents also have some action in repelling flies, gnats, and mosquitoes. When mixing the sprays intended for horses, be sure to use the dilutions for spraying on animals, not premises. Stick to veterinary products. Products intended for humans may have high concentrations of DEET, and may be toxic to animals.

After a trip, I bathe my dogs with a flea and tick shampoo before taking them in the house. Shampoos have very little residual action, which means once they are off the dog, they are no longer doing anything to prevent infestation. Pyrethrin sprays also have little residual action. Organophosphate dips have a much greater residual action, but considerably greater potential for toxicity. Consult your veterinarian about the use of these products.

Products intended for humans may be toxic to animals.

Encountering Other Animals

Rabies

While fleas and ticks are a nuisance, one of the greatest dangers your dog could face is a meeting with another animal. As mentioned before, every state requires that dogs be vaccinated against rabies. This law is for your animal's protection, as well as that of others.

Rabies occurs in all mammals, but in the United States the greatest danger is posed by four animals: the raccoon, the skunk, the bat, and the fox.

Previously, different areas of the country had different animals that maintained the reservoir of the disease in that region; but due to transportation of wild animals, any of these animals, in any part of the country, should be considered a risk.

Keep your dog's rabies vaccinations current, and familiarize yourself with local rabies laws. The following are the recommendations of the National Association of Public Health Veterinarians, while they may or may not be law where you live, it is best to act as if they were.

Keep your dog's rabies vaccination current.

- If a dog is bitten or scratched by a wild animal that is not available for rabies testing, the dog is regarded as having been exposed to rabies.
- If the dog has been vaccinated previously, the recommendation is to revaccinate and observe him for ninety days.
- If the dog is not currently vaccinated, the recommendation is for immediate euthanasia and testing for rabies.

When the owner is unwilling to have this done, the animal should be placed in strict isolation for six months, and vaccinated one month prior to release. (Note that the isolation is at the owner's expense. If your dog bites someone, your life will be made a great deal easier if the animal has been vaccinated.)

If your dog has an encounter with a wild animal, report it to your veterinarian immediately. While in the field, you can clean out the dog's wound with copious amounts of water, using soap or Betadine. The wound is also susceptible to bacterial infection. As your dog may object to having a wound scrubbed, be sure to muzzle him for your own protection. Though it is unlikely that saliva (the body fluid responsible for transmission of rabies) remaining in the dog's wound is infectious, I recommend that you wear latex gloves while cleaning the wound.

Porcupines

Your dog jaunts off into the woods and comes back with a face full of quills. He has quills in his nose, his cheeks, and even his mouth. There is no need to panic, but the trip is over and it's time for a visit to the veterinarian. Interestingly enough, it seems that certain dogs get porcupined over and over again.

Skunks

Though important vectors of rabies, skunks are of course more notorious for their ability to thwart agressors by spraying them with the contents of their anal sacs. A sprayed dog is intolerable. Tomato juice, the traditional remedy, has mixed reviews in its efficacy at removing the stink. There are chemical descenting solutions that you can obtain at pet supply stores or at a veterinarian's office.

Handling Medical Emergencies

A Scenario

You're hiking on a long distance trail and your dog has taken a spill. A bone is poking through her skin, and she is breathing rapidly. It's 8:30 in the evening as you make it to the nearest road. You know that there is a hospital in the county and you flag down a passing car. The driver says that there may be a veterinarian in the next town, but he's not sure. You're nervous because your dog's pulse is getting weak and her gums are pretty white. You get to the next town where there is a veterinarian, but he's closed. At a pay phone, a quarter-mile down the road, you dial his emergency number, only to find that on this night he is referring his emergencies to a clinic fifteen miles away. The kind soul who picked you up has since left. And there you are, sitting at a payphone with a dog in need of medical care, and no idea where to go.

Chances are good that you won't ever be in this situation. But preparedness for wilderness and backcountry trips means forseeing the scenarios that could produce difficulty. What I hope to illustrate by this anecdote is that in backcountry hiking, you will be putting your dog in situations where, if worse comes to worst, you will be unable to help him. That's a risk that we take when we head into the woods. Let that be a conscious decision, not a sad realization if you find yourself and your dog in a life-threatening dilemma.

Preparedness for backcountry trips means forseeing scenarios that could produce difficulty.

There are many places where veterinary care is sparse to non-existent.

Some people avoid extended trips away from "civilization" because of what they feel is inadequate medical care. When backpacking with your dog, be aware that you are separating him from medical facilities, perhaps to an even greater degree than yourself. There are many places where veterinary care is sparse to non-existent. I assume the reader is aware of this fact and will do all he or she can to prevent medical emergencies. Be willing to accept the responsibility of placing your animal in a dangerous situation.

Wilderness first aid courses for humans are now offered in many places. Many of the same principles apply to canine first aid. For the day hiker, much of this information is superfluous—in an emergency, it would be better just to get out and get to the nearest veterinarian. For the trekker heading into remote wildernesses for extended periods of time, one of these first aid courses, along with consulting your veterinarian as to how these practices can best be adapted to animals, is recommended.

Do you know how to perform cardiopulmonary resuscitation on a dog, and are you willing to do so? Is the sight of an open wound going to make you swoon? These are things to consider before you hit the trail.

Although disaster rarely happens, think ahead and consider how you would handle it with your dog. Try to imagine every situation that you'll be putting your dog in. Will you have to leave him in the truck somewhere when it's ninety-five degrees in the shade? Are you travelling through snake country? If the scenario is too scary, maybe a shorter trip or a dog-sitter is in order.

Pain

This is probably as good a time as any to make a note on dogs in pain. Dogs in pain cannot be relied upon to act as they normally would. This means that your most loyal, obedient friend might bite you as you attempt to help her. It's a natural pain response, so don't take it personally. If you are bitten, there are now two injuries to deal with instead of one.

Dogs in pain can not be relied upon to act as they normally would.

A muzzle will prevent your dog from biting you, and, in many cases, will actually lessen his anxiety. You can use a light store-bought muzzle made out of nylon, or a strip of fabric or gauze. If you have brought cravats for your own medical kit, those will serve quite well.

Make a loop with the strip of fabric, putting the overhand knot above the dog's muzzle. Tighten. Then cross the ends underneath the dog's jaw and tie the muzzle behind the dog's ears. Don't be afraid to tighten this thing—the skin you save will be your own.

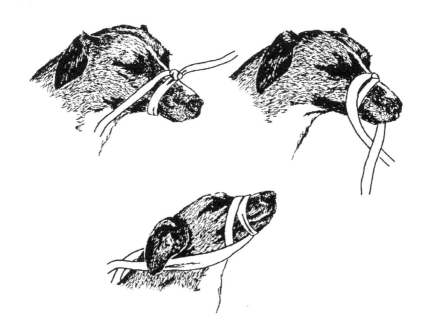

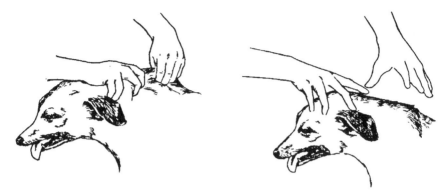

Dehydration

A bugaboo for both human and canine travellers, too little water in the system poses a serious threat to the health of the camper. Dehydration can be the result of either inadequate intake or excessive loss of fluids. For dogs, a large amount of water can be lost panting to keep cool.

A large amount of water can be lost panting to keep cool.

"Skin tenting" is a crude way to estimate a dog's hydration status. The skin above the shoulder blades is lifted, then dropped. A well-hydrated dog's skin will drop immediately back in place. If a dog is 5-10 percent dehydrated, the skin will sink slowly. Try this on your dog under normal conditions.

Look at your dog's gums. They should be moist and pink, except for those dogs that have some pigment on their gums. If the gums are tacky, or dry and dark, you've got problems. Give your dog as much to drink as possible, and evacuate for further medical care. Dehydration has all sorts of consequences that may require hospitalization.

A vomiting dog, or a dog with severe diarrhea, is prone to dehydration, as vast amounts of fluids can be lost from either end. After a dog vomits, she tends to drink water, which causes more vomiting and an actual increase in the amount of fluid loss. In a hospital setting, this problem is remedied by giving the dog fluids intravenously and administering medicine that reduces vomiting. In the field, one has to tread a line between letting the dog drink and vomit itself to dehydration, or dehydrating the dog by withholding water. In general, it is best to wait until the dog has not vomited for several hours, then offer small amounts of water. If these are tolerated, offer increasing amounts. Food should be withheld until the vomiting has stopped for at least twenty-four hours.

Heat Stroke

Heat stroke is one form of hyperthermia, a life-threatening condition in which the body's temperature reaches a level incompatible with normal life functions. Virtually every system in the body is affected, as your animal stews in his own juices.

Heat stroke is nearly always preventable. You all know it, but the classic case of a dog with hyperthermia is the poor canine whose owner has shut him up in the car, windows closed, on a hot summer day. *Never leave your dog in a hot car during the day!* This means anything above 65° F. Hyperthermia sets in amazingly fast. You could run into the store for "just a minute," and return to a medical emergency.

Never leave your dog in a hot car during the day!

Hyperthermia can also result when a dog is not acclimated to hot temperatures. Do you live in an air-conditioned environment? Water deprivation, obesity, and exercise can lead to hyperthermia as well. High humidity makes things worse, as does having a dog who is out of shape. Therefore, the weekend warrior's dog, who is not getting adequate exercise, and is subjected to a forced march with inadequate water, is our classic victim.

A dog will generally begin panting and showing signs of discomfort prior to going into heat stroke.

Go at the dog's pace rather than your own.

The key is to go at the dog's pace rather than your own. Most dogs, when feeling overheated, will head for the shade, lie down and pant, and show a reluctance to continue. Take the hint. Give him some water and take a break.

If you have a thermometer in your first aid kit (a digital rectal thermometer is light and cheap), you can determine your dog's temperature. Normal temperature in a dog is 100.5-102.5° F, but an excited or recently-exercised animal may register slightly higher without any cause for concern.

A temperature of higher than 106° F calls for aggressive cooling. Extreme panting, excessive salivation, darkened or bright red mucous membranes (look in the dog's mouth) are all signs of hyperthermia. The dog may collapse or become comatose; heart rate will be increased; the urine may have the color of machine oil.

Treatment for hyperthermia is immersion in cold water, or spraying with cold water if immersion is not possible. Ice and snow can have a counterproductive effect, causing blood vessels near the skin to shut down, preventing the skin from acting as a radiator. If you have a thermometer, cease cooling when the dog's temperature has reached 103° F.

Heat stroke is an emergency evacuation situation. Even though the dog's temperature has been brought down to normal, there are still dangers due to the damage done by the high temperature. Hospitalization will be necessary.

Once again, it's hard to imagine a situation in which heat stroke cannot be prevented. Excepting the worst of luck, the well-prepared camper will never see this condition.

Cuts and Abrasions

These are relatively common injuries in dogs. Often cuts are caused by man-made objects—a piece of barbed wire or a carelessly discarded bottle.

A cut pad will bleed like the dickens. Frequently, a cut will look a lot worse than it is, due to the volume of blood present. The best way to stop bleeding is direct pressure and elevation. This isn't as easy with dogs as it is with humans. Many times an animal will resist direct pressure on an injury, as well as being turned on her back.

The best way to stop bleeding is with direct pressure and elevation.

Don't worry about dog blood. Veterinarians do not routinely wear latex gloves when dealing with dog blood, and the lack of gloves should not prevent you from attempting to stem the flow of blood from your dog's wound. Cleanse the wound, and check it for the presence of foreign objects.

In a hospital setting, the wound area is routinely clipped to keep hair away from it, but this will be difficult to do in the field. If the wound is full of dirt and debris, a jet of water is best for cleansing it. A large 60 cc dosing syringe is good for this purpose, but so is a bicycle-type water bottle. This should be followed by washing with a povidone-iodine solution, such as Betadine—alcohol will just make the wound sting.

Bandaging

You should have some sterile dressings to place over a wound.

A wound should be covered to keep it as clean as possible, and to prevent further injury and hemorrhage. As part of your own medical kit, you should have some sterile dressings to place over a wound. These should be covered by some type of non-sterile bandage.

Nearly anything you have in your backpack can be used to make a bandage. Clothing cut into strips works well. I generally take an Ace bandage and some Vet-Wrap tape in my medical kit; these can be used on my dogs or myself. Vet-Wrap is a cohesive tape, which means that it sticks to itself but not to skin. It makes a nice covering for most types of dressing.

Both Vet-Wrap tape and Ace bandages are made of stretchy material, so you should be careful when using them on limbs, especially near the feet. They have a tendency to tighten, cutting off circulation below the bandage. Whenever you put a bandage around a dog's leg, check the limb frequently for swelling, coldness, loss of sensation, or pain.

Trauma

The most likely time for trauma to occur is when your dog is crossing a road. Many of these injuries are fatal, or become so, given the remoteness of the surroundings. Check your maps and trail guides for road crossings. If your dog is leashed, roads are not a danger.

Dogs do slip and fall, drown, or get impaled on objects, and they can always find new and creative ways to hurt themselves. The idea that Mother Nature's creatures instinctively avoid hurt is simply not true. Do not carry your dog in the back of a pickup truck.

Lameness

Animals limp when they've been hurt. We call it lameness. Lameness can be caused by something as simple as a sore foot, or something more serious, such as a complex fracture of a limb.

With a limping dog, in the absence of an obvious deformity (like that bullet hole in the upper foreleg), check the feet first. Owners will observe a limping dog and wonder whether an elbow, a shoulder, or a hip has been injured. Often, it's nothing more than a sharp stone or thorn wedged between the foot pads. Separate the pads and feel with your fingers. Removal of the offending object usually brings immediate relief.

If the lameness isn't caused by a cut pad, or a sore foot, the problem may be musculoskeletal in nature. These injuries range from sprains and strains to angulated fractures with protruding bones. When your dog shows signs of pain—anything from looking and licking nervously at a site on her body to howling—it's time to investigate.

A careful physical examination will usually tell you what the problem is. Since your dog can't tell

When your dog shows signs of pain, it's time to investigate.

you what's the matter, you are going to have to use your eyes and hands to figure out what's wrong. This means pulling and squeezing body parts. The dog will respond by showing pain—turning her head, withdrawing the limb, vocalizing. Watch out that you don't get bitten!

Performing a physical exam on a dog takes experience and practice. It is beyond the range of this volume to undertake that topic. However, the owner who is willing to examine his dog, will generally be able to help his animal sooner than the one who relies on the nearest veterinarian.

Broken bones will have swelling around them, and you can usually feel and hear crepitus—a grinding sensation and sound—as the bone ends scrape against each other. A piece of bone sticking through the skin is another obvious sign of breakage.

Sometimes, you'll be confused. Your dog will exhibit tenderness in a limb, although you didn't see any injury occur. A dog with a torn cruciate ligament, for example, will limp, and you may not be able to localize the pain.

If your dog is limping, remove her pack to lessen the load.

If your dog is limping, remove her pack to lessen the load. Provided that the pain isn't too great, or if the injury is limited to one leg, she can limp her way homeward. If the lameness is on two legs, and it's severe, at least one of those legs is going to bear the brunt of further travel. At this point, consider carrying your dog for at least part of the distance.

Cold almost always helps in the initial twenty-four hours after a musculoskeletal injury. If you have ice packs or some other way of applying cold to the injured area, you can do so for fifteen minutes at a time, as tolerated. In addition, rest will help injuries.

There is a temptation to give medication to relieve a dog's discomfort. Pain relievers are a double-edged sword when treating animals: You want to ease your dog's pain, but that pain prevents him from further injuring himself. Aspirin can be given, with food, at the rate of one aspirin per seventy pound dog twice a day. Do not use products containing ibuprofen or acetominophen! (And for those of you with cats, use none of these.) Aspirin has the same side effects in dogs as it does in humans. Using it to get a dog through a trip instead of evacuating is poor judgment.

Pain prevents him from further injuring himself.

Broken Bones

A broken limb should be splinted. A splint does not provide your dog a way to walk out of the wilderness—it provides a degree of stability that will prevent further injury and gives some relief from pain.

Splinting principles are simple. For a broken bone, we splint the joint above and the joint below the break. For an injured joint, we splint the long bone above and the long bone below.

A good splint has several features. First of all, it will be comfortable to the wearer. Depending on what you are using for the splint—a smooth piece of wood, an Insulite pad rolled to make it stiff, a tent pole, etc.—it needs to be well-padded at its contact points in order to prevent sores from developing. Secondly, it must provide stability. If the splint is flopping around, it could do more harm than good. Thirdly, the splint places the limb in a "normal" position—the broken bone in line, and the joints in a neutral position. Finally, splints need to be checked frequently to make sure that they are working and doing no harm.

Splints need to be checked frequently.

Previous practice was to splint angulated fractures "as they lay." In a wilderness setting, it is now considered both proper and necessary to put fractures into normal anatomical positions before splinting, both for the comfort of the animal and for the preservation of the limb. Again, be aware of your comfort level—your dog may not cooperate, and you may not be comfortable with what you are doing. Educating yourself by talking to your veterinarian, and taking a wilderness medical course, will increase your comfort level.

Snakebites

Most snake bites are not witnessed. They generally occur on the face, reflecting a dog's way of approaching the world nose-first.

A snake bite will usually have two puncture wounds, surrounded by lots of swelling. The injury will be accompanied by significant pain. Often there will be bleeding around the wound site.

Keep the dog calm and evacuate to the nearest medical care.

Keeping the dog calm and evacuating her to the nearest medical care is the treatment for snake bites. Cutting the wound and sucking out the venom is not a good idea. It may calm you to know that evenomation occurs in less than half of all snake bites.

Once under the care of a veterinarian, your dog will be given antivenin, if needed, along with supportive care. Allergic reactions to antivenin are rare among dogs. The most common problem with snakebite is tissue sloughing in the weeks subsequent to the bite.

Shock

Shock is not the horror that you feel on discovering a large gash in your side. It is the medical problem resulting from all that blood pouring out of the gash. Shock, in medical terms, means you are not getting enough blood to your tissues. This situation is eventually incompatible with life when it affects your brain or your heart.

Shock means you are not getting enough blood to your tissues.

In its early stages, shock will be manifested by increased respiratory and heart rates, followed in its later stages by slowed respirations and a decreased heart rate. The pulse will be weak.

A good place to take a dog's pulse is on the inside of the thigh, on the femoral artery. Practice doing this under normal circumstances when checking your dog, so that you will know how to find his pulse. If you are used to examining your dog, you will be more aware of what normal is.

Other signs of shock will be white gums and mucous membranes, slow capillary refill time, reduced urine output, hypothermia, and possibly coma. Fixed, dilated pupils are not a good sign. Capillary refill time is observed by pressing on the gums so that they blanche, and seeing how long it takes for the blanched area to turn pink again. Normal is one to one-and-one-half seconds. Try this on your dog to see what normal is.

While in the field, treatment for shock is difficult at best. If you are carrying your dog in a litter, a head down position is preferred. There are various types of body wrappings that supposedly keep the blood at the body's core and flowing to the brain, but their use is of questionable efficacy. Beating a hasty retreat to the nearest veterinary clinic is the only way to deal with life-threatening shock. Shock is a killer, and in a remote location, there will be little you can do about it.

Milder degrees of shock often resolve on their own, as the body reabsorbs blood from a cavity, or the problems with the blood vessels correct themselves. You will not necessarily be able to determine the severity of the shock by the nature of the injury. Immediate evacuation is still the dog's only hope if the shock is severe or progressive.

Shock is a killer, and in a remote location, there will be little you can do about it.

CPR

Cardiopulmonary resuscitation (CPR) is used to maintain basic life systems until advanced life support can be established. This is true for humans, as well as dogs. Instruction is necessary for all forms of CPR; your veterinarian should be able to teach you the proper technique for administering CPR to your dog. But, if your dog needs CPR, don't let lack of training stop you from trying. Six hours from the trailhead you don't have much choice. It's also a bad time to try and learn.

The indication for CPR is lack of a heartbeat and lack of breathing. In other words, administer CPR when the dog appears to be dead. If your dog has even a slight heartbeat, do not attempt chest compressions. If the dog has a heartbeat, but is not breathing, rescue breathing should be started.

Mouth-to-nose breathing is the canine equivilent of mouth-to-mouth.

Rescue breathing, or mouth-to-nose breathing, is the canine-human equivalent of mouth-to-mouth breathing. When assessing an unconscious animal, the ABC system is used:

A-Is there an Airway?

B-Is the dog Breathing?

C-Circulation: Does the dog have a pulse?

If the dog is not breathing, attempt a couple of

ventilations. This is done by placing your mouth over the dog's nose and exhaling. If the chest doesn't rise, check in the dog's mouth for debris that could be obstructing the airway. Pull his tongue forward and close his mouth with the tongue between the front teeth; try again. If nothing is going in, it is possible that something has lodged in the airway.

It is possible that something has lodged in the airway.

The Heimlich maneuver can be performed on a dog by positioning him on his side and pressing behind the rib cage. For smaller dogs, you can use the same method used on human infants: cradle them in a head down position and deliver several blows between the shoulder blades. Once an airway has been established, the dog will either breath on his own, or you will need to continue mouth-to-nose resuscitation.

Check for a pulse. If there is no pulse, begin chest compressions. These are done with the dog lying on his side. By placing your thumb on the dog's elbow, your hand will be in the proper position for compressions. Compressions should be done at the rate of 80-120 per minute. The amount of the compression will depend on the size of the dog. A large dog will require both hands pressing down about two inches, whereas a toy breed will require only two fingers compressing about one-half inch. If you are by yourself, give two breaths for every fifteen compressions; give one breath for every five compressions if there are two of you.

Don't expect miracles. For all its publicity, CPR actually saves very few lives. In most cases, its success is related to the immediate availability of advanced life support. CPR will be more useful in a case of drowning or electrocution than in a case of shock, where the problem is on-going and will not be corrected by the CPR.

If you are reading this section for the first time

with a dying dog in front of you, it's too late. If the preceding description has been confusing, that's because CPR is a skill that requires practice. Ask your veterinarian how to perform CPR on a canine. This, in conjunction with a human CPR course, will give you greater confidence if you are faced with a situation that requires CPR.

Evacuation

In the event that your dog needs emergency evacuation, you will need to devise some way to carry her. The evacuation of a large dog is going to present a significant challenge. It is unlikely that people will be able to lug a St. Bernard for any measurable distance. Smaller animals, like my forty to forty-five pounders, fit conveniently in a backpack with their heads sticking out (though they object strongly). A dog can be carried around your neck, torso over the back of the neck, front legs and back legs coming down on opposite sides of your chest.

The evacuation of a large dog is going to present a significant challenge.

A dog with back injuries should be placed on his side on a board, but boards are hardly standard backcountry equipment. The most common back injuries causing neurological signs in dogs are ruptured disks which impinge on the spinal cord. The faster they are dealt with, the greater chance the dog has of a full and complete recovery.

Euthanasia

When an animal has suffered an injury that is incompatible with life, choosing a more rapid death is often the final gift of love that an owner can bestow. There are many ways of killing an animal quickly, but owners will vary in their ability to administer a quick, painless death in a way that they find acceptable. Euthanasia should be looked upon as the absence of pain and the absence of fear. Consider this possibility before taking your dog on a dangerous trip.

Conclusion

This book is a study in avoiding problems and how to deal with them once they occur. There is little room to expand on how much fun it is to get out with your dog—to see the outdoors not only with human eyes, but also in that special way a dog has of looking at the world.

There is little room to expand on the fun it is to get out with your dog.

My intention is to help the hiker plan a safe trip and be able to deal with problems if something does not go as planned. I hope to have chipped away at the "Let's just throw 'em in the back of the truck and head on out" type of mentality, and to have instilled a bit of respect for the dangers that dogs might face on the trail.

Fortuitously for dogs and their owners, most

trips occur without mishap, and most of this book will be just for the sake of teaching that respect. My greater purpose is to help dog owners discover the pleasure that I have gotten from having journeyed with my animals. The human-canine bond is enhanced by these journeys, and I imagine my dogs feel the same way.

Additional Reading

I have avoided including training books. There are so many on the market, each touting a system preferred by the different authors, that making a choice is a daunting task. Personally, I have found obedience courses quite useful.

Many dog books center on the characteristics and qualities of different breeds. In no way is a purebred dog necessarily superior to mixed breed for purposes of hiking. In addition, mixed breed dogs are less apt to suffer from the problems of inbreeding. Be aware of this when reading a dog book that stresses breeds. Some books on general dog care are listed below.

Caras, Roger, *A Dog is Listening*. Summit Books, NY 1992

Fogle, Bruce, *101 Questions Your Dog Would Ask Its Vet*. Carroll and Graf, NY 1993

Gerstenfeld, Sheldon, *The Dog Care Book*. Addison-Wesley, CA 1989

Hawcroft, Tim, *First Aid for Dogs*. Howell Book House, NY 1994

Humphries, Jim, *Dr. Jim's Animal Clinic for Dogs*. Howell Book House, NY 1994

McGinnis, Terri, *The Well Dog Book*. Random House, NY 1991

Taylor, David, *You and Your Dog*. Knopf, NY 1994